The Credit Investor

Corey P Smith

Library of Congress Catalog Card Number: On File

Library of Congress Control Number: On File

Printed in the United States of America

Editor: Chandra Sparks Taylor, www.chandrasparkstaylor.com
Cover design: Felix Walker
Book design: Essex Graphix, www.essexgraphix.com

The Credo Company
4466 Elvis Presley Blvd., Ste. 260
Memphis, TN 38116
coreysmith1793@gmail.com
www.coreypsmith.com

Table of Contents

Disclaimer

This publication is designed to provide accurate and authoritative information with regard to the subject matter covered. While all of the stories described in the book are based on true experiences, most of the names are pseudonyms, and some situations have been changed slightly for educational purposes and to protect each individual's privacy. It is sold with the understanding that the publisher is not engaged in rendering legal or other professional advice. If legal advice or other expert assistance is required, the services of a competent professional person should be sought.

The authors and publishers specifically disclaim all responsibility for any liability, loss, or risk, personal or otherwise, which is incurred as a consequence, directly or indirectly, of the use and application of any of the contents of this book. The Credo Company, its Logo and Marks, are trademarks of The Credo Company LLC.

Authors Statement

There are many people who think they know what a credit investor or credit partner really is, but they do not. As you begin to read this book it will become clear to you who the credit investors truly are and the power that they hold. Nevertheless, it is up to you to find a way to manipulate this chess game of life so that you can become something more than a pawn.

If you have read any of my other books, such as Conspiracy of Credit, The Game of Credit, The Credit Dictionary, or Credit Is For Poor People, you may remember me talking about how the idea of credit investor really resonated in my mind in a way that I could become one man, but yet using many people. What does this mean? This simply means duplicating myself through other people. It hit me one day when I was sitting at a red light and saw a homeless man and I asked myself," who has more to loss, myself or the homeless man." Of course, the answer was me! The reason I said me, was because the homeless man had nothing to lose, he had already lost everything, but one thing that he had not loss was the first gift in life, which was his name.

You see the one thing that we all start out with in life is our name. Some people name automatically carries more value and power than others depending on their family tree. But one thing that I knew that the homeless man was like a newborn baby and could be made into anybody I wanted him to be at this point. Some of the things that I had to consider were the characteristics of a homeless person and so, I had to be careful about my approach to any homeless person with a business proposition. Not only that, but it also had to be the right person, meaning they still had to be in their right mind and possibly not on drugs.

One thing about homeless people is that they may have poor attention span, poor self-esteem, extreme shyness and most of all difficulty trusting people. This is why I said my approach had to be a cautious one, because gaining their trust is the most important thing. Trust is important because most homeless people will not have a birth certificate, drivers license or social security card and you will need to obtain these, if you plan on using them as credit investors. Now don't get me wrong, it is not just about utilizing homeless people or should I say partnering up with them to become credit investors, but it's about finding any person who does not understand the power of their name.

Remember what I said, by the time you finish reading this book you will understand who the true credit investors are because at the end of the day credit investing is simply about debt and whoever can invest in the most debt, will be and is the biggest credit investor. What does that mean Corey P. Smith? Continue to read and I will explain.

Economics And Credit

The power of Economics and Credit is unmatched when it comes to the financial status of rich people and poor people. But one of them affects rich people and the other effects poor people. Economics is a social science that studies how people and societies produce, distribute, and consume goods and services. It examines how people respond to incentives and make decisions. Credit on the other hand is a person's history of borrowing and repaying money. In other words, it is one's ability to manage debt.

You see, when we talk about economics and we focus on those words produce and distribute, we are talking about the rich and their ability to control consumer goods and services. So, credit and the ability or inability to manage debt refers to the poor. The reason I wanted to explain this is because there is an industry known as Credit Investor or what some have come to know as Credit Partners. Now some people may simply think that a credit investor is one individual or company using someone else's personal credit as a means of leverage in the absence of capital. Well, let me explain what a true credit investor is and how it has evolved over the years.

A credit investor is someone who invests in debt securities or loans issued by governments or corporations. Credit investors are essentially lending money to the issuer in exchange for interest payments and the return of the principal amount at maturity.

Credit investors are creditors, not owners, of the issuing company. They have a legal claim for the payments, but do not participate in the company's management or decision making. Some examples of credit investments include loans, bonds, which can be issued by governments or corporations, investment notes and bank loans. Does any of the loans sound familiar?

Credit investing comprises two types of investments (debt and equity) and involves investing in credit or a debt loan. Credit investments can take several forms, including consumer and small business loans, venture debt, specialty loans and other forms of private debt. I would like you to consider the last form of debt, called private debt. I would like you to consider the last form of debt, called private debt. Think about this a "collection debt" is considered a private debt when it is handled by a private collection agency, which is a third-party company contracted by the original creditor to collect on an outstanding debt. Another example of this would be unpaid taxes that are managed by the IRS, where private collection agencies are used to pursue overdue tax bills on the government's behalf. So, think about this, the biggest credit investor is also the biggest collection agency.

The reason why I explained the difference between economics and credit is because the relationship between economics and credit is because the relationship between economics and rich people is complex. Rich people can stimulate economic growth, or they can stunt economic growth. The reason why, is because the concentration of wealth can be harmful. They can do this through the controlling the stock market, corporate power because they can influence to oppose labor laws and policies that benefit the working class, they can also fight minimum wage increase through political restrictions and remember when I said, "the concentration of wealth can be harmful." I made this statement because the concentration of wealth can undermine efforts to reduce poverty, discrimination and gender equality.

Rich people affect economics and economics affect credit. Economics impact credit by influencing the availability and cost of borrowing through factors like interest rates, which are set by central banks based on economic conditions, meaning a healthy economy generally provides easier access to credit at lower interest rates, while a struggling economy can lead to tighter credit availability and higher interest rates, potentially impacting ones ability to borrow money for major purchases like homes or cars. All of this sounds good, but who determines all of these factors? THE RICH!

The one key thing you must see in all of this is the Central Bank determines all of these factors. The Federal Reserve Board (FRB) governs the Federal Reserve System, and the U.S. Central Bank. The Federal Reserve Bank is part of the Federal Open Market Committee (FOMC), which includes five of the twelve regional bank presidents on a rotating basis. The FOMC determines the direction of monetary policy. The Federal Reserve Bank also works with the Reserve bank, which are private corporations that serve banks, the US Treasury, and the public. Remember when I stated part of controlling economics is through corporate power? Well, let me point this statement out again, "Private Corporations That Serve Banks."

I have always said that in order to defeat anything, you must know and understand its origin. This is my reason for breaking down economics and credit as it relates to who are the true credit investors of the world. Once I understood all of these things, that is when I truly had to figure out how to manipulate the system to benefit me financially.

Pawns In the Game

You ever wonder why almost everything is based off numbers, or some type of grade. Better yet, they want you to conduct a survey to rate something whether it is a product, food, hotel or just your experience with something.

I titled this chapter Pawns In The Game for a reason, and that reason is to explain the association between credit and education But, first let me explain to you exactly the purpose of a pawn in the game of chess and the purpose of education as it relates to shaping your thinking.

You see, a pawn is considered the weakest piece in chess because it has minimal movement powers. They are never seen as a piece that is used for attacking or capturing a bigger piece and their lifespan is very short on the board. They are often used to shield more powerful pieces; therefore they are sacrificed a lot. This almost sound like a human being who can't think for themselves, have very little money and resources, nor does the world place a lot of value on their life.

Now let me explain to you why the education piece is so important when it comes to how you think, how you act, and how you move throughout your life. That means chasing your dreams or being the pawn in someone else's dream.

The modern-day public school system was started from one of the biggest Public Relations campaigns ever and it was all because of one man and his name was John D. Rockefeller. He was the biggest oil tycoons at the time controlling more than 90% of the oil in the United States and his net worth was about 418 billion when adjusted for today's inflation rate. Because of the lack of wealth equality, he decided to donate one million dollars to the General Board of Education, which is equivalent to about twenty five million dollars in today's inflation rate.

Rockefeller was not out to make the public more educated; his intent was to make the public into a good work force. He said, "I don't want a nation of thinkers, I want a nation of workers." That statement right there should tell you a lot about the thinking of Rockefeller and those like him as it came to perception of the poor. You see, Rockefeller had a friend named Abraham Flexner and his philosophy was when you write the books you control exactly what is being taught and what is being learned. The point that I am trying to make is once the Board of Education and the school system was fully underway, the dumbing down of the American public was in full effect. Therefore, it became easy to create the pawns in the game. Let me explain how this works in the world of credit.

I want you to think about something, in school you receive an A through F depending on your score, in credit you receive a rating based on a score, if you take an uber or Lyft, they want you to rate the driver by giving one or five stars. Two of these situations are private, while one is public. Basically, what is happening in all these situations is punishing the bad and rewarding the good. This is basically a social ranking system applied for various reasons on various levels of society. Both the private and public sector are utilizing social ranking systems as a mechanism to engineer human behavior, creating a form of digitally induced social control.

Believe it or not, social scoring systems have been around for decades. In the past social scoring was based on status, origin, resources, family ties, and education. Eventually financial institutions and credit firms started using complex data streams to assess payment risk and provide loans to consumers based on their assessment. Now get this, credit firms have identified the benefit of using information about one's social network to assess risk. It seems that the people you associate with are key indicators of your own behavior. "Bird of a feather flock together."

Demographic and behavioral data is used in this modern-day social ranking system. Remember in my book "How to Outsmart The Credit Bureaus" I told you how Experian was using census tracts and geographical codes to assist the lending institutions with red lining. It is now possible to use various data sources and sophisticated techniques and technology to determine one's position within a social system. This creates new ways of utilizing social ranking mechanisms in the online world, far beyond the realm of loan provisioning.

All of the things that have become common in our lives and that we use every day, such as social media sites, mobile apps, hospitality providers, travel organizations, and television apps readily use social ranking systems to help categorize products, services, and experiences.

One thing that many of us do not understand is businesses, the government, and public institutions are showing a deep interest in the application of online social ranking systems. Remember Rockefeller said, "He wanted a nation of workers," and he began by investing in education. The purpose of a social credit system is to socially engineer acceptable behaviors, promote good conduct, and control a society based on the norms and values governing its systems.

Think about that, "the norms and values governing a system." Remember when I told you that Abraham Flexner believes that, if you wrote the books, then you could control the education and what is being taught. That's the governing system that we now live in every day. It has been intensified, due to technology.

The only way for you to play the game and not remain a pawn is to educate yourself, move how you want to move and not be used as a puppet for those in power.

Becoming The Credit Investor

The most important thing to remember when dealing with your own credit investor or partner is contracts and agreements. Contracts are important because they clearly define the terms and expectations of an agreement between you, the business and the credit investor. This will minimize the risk of misunderstandings and disputes, protecting the interest of everybody involved. I had to learn this early on because one of my credit investors did not want to be honest with their spouse.

Let me tell you a story about how a contract and credit investor agreement protected me when the law came knocking. In 2007, I entered into a credit investor agreement with a young lady that I had known from a previous girlfriend. She had excellent credit; in fact, her credit scores range from 747 to 770 across the board. Remember that not only having contracts and agreements are good, but also having copies of the credit investors' identification, birth certificate and social security card are also very important.

Initially, me and this young lady talked about how we would do the splits on any loans, credit cards or lines of credit that were obtained. She told me that she really needed money to invest in rental properties. Normally when I discuss percentages with credit investors, it is a 85 percent to the company and 15 percent to the investor. The reason the percentages are done this way is because most credit investors do not have the initial seed money to set a company up and make sure that is has everything it needs in order to have a bigger appearance than what it really is, especially with the underwriters. But, due to the history of my relationship with this young lady and because I really did not have to do any work on her credit, I agreed to a 50/50 split.

The first thing that I did was purchase a Shelf Corporation and made her the principal officer in the company. I also paid for a brick and mortar office and three years tax returns to go along with the Shelf Corporation. Now keep in mind this was twenty years ago, and things were a lot cheaper and simpler. However, I made sure that the company had a corporate address, phone number, fax, website, 800 number in addition to local phone number. I also made sure the company was registered with the Better Business Bureau, Chamber of Commerce and a member of at least one charity organization. Today, I make sure that all the social media outlets are included in the list.

Then next thing that I did was have all of the credit investors mail forwarded to an address that I had complete control over, and it is a must that whatever mailing address that you mail forwarded to, you should have the credit investor go and change their identification or drivers license to reflect the updated address. The reason I do this is because I did not want to waste my time and money on a Shelf Corporation or credit investor and not benefit in the end. This can happen sometimes, if they start feeling like they are the reason everything is happening.

The laws have changed when it comes to mail forwarding because now when you forward any US mail, you must show identification, such as a drivers license. Nevertheless, once I have a complete profile established on my new credit investor, I make sure that all of the contracts were transparent between both parties. One other thing that I required was for the credit investor to provide me with a single photo of themselves, usually one that I would take. I also ask that they provide me with two pieces of mail from their home. This was usually a bank statement and a utility bill, if this was a credit investor that was not homeless. All of this will make sense once I finish explaining to you what happened.

Once I started to acquire funding from different banks and credit cards, things were looking promising. Back around 2005 up until 2008 banks were very friendly to small businesses. I mean you could easily get approved for a fifty-thousand-dollar line of credit without documentation. This was basically called a stated income loan. Needless to say, I had accumulated about $425,000 with the credit investor and everything was going as planned. Remember that I told you that I knew my credit investor from a previous relationship and that she did not want to be honest with her spouse.

Well one afternoon, her husband was home from work early and the bank called. The name of the bank was First Tennessee Bank and they told her husband they were calling regarding a payment that was due on a $50,000 line of credit that her company had received. Well, of course her husband had no idea that his wife had a $50,000 dollar line of credit with First Tennessee Bank and so he told the customer service agent that they had the wrong person. The customer service agent told him that in fact they had the right person. This made her husband curious and mad at the same time because he knew nothing about his wife doing business with First Tennessee Bank and getting a $50,000 dollar line of credit. When his wife got home, he began to question her, and she denied. And because she denied it, he wanted her to go and file a police report. So, this is exactly what the wife did, all because she did not want to tell her husband the truth.

Remember that I told you that I would make my credit investors principal officers of the Shelf Corporation. Well, I still would be listed as a signer on the accounts or an officer on the operating agreement. The more her husband questioned her, the more she gave in to his demands. Eventually her denial turned into an even bigger lie, and that lie was that I stole her identity. You see where this is going and why I say contracts, agreements, and other paperwork are so important. After she went down to the police department and filed an identity theft report on me, this led to a series of events that ultimately led to her being arrested for filing a false police report.

I pulled up at home one day around three o'clock one day and I received a couple of calls from a 636 number. Immediately, I knew this number because I had already been through some issues with the Economic Crimes Bureau of the Memphis Police Department. So, the third time they called back I answered and it was a female detective on the other end. I asked her, "how can I help you," and she responds by saying that she was about to put a warrant out for my arrest for identity theft and fraud. I asked, "her who identity did I steal?" She responded by telling me my credit investor name. And so, I paused for a minute, and then I told her that I have nothing to say or talk about! She says to me, "Why don't you want to talk, sounds like a guilty man to me," and I respond by telling her, "Sounds like a smart man to me, and like I said, I have nothing to say." Then I said, "Give me your number and I will have my attorney call you." The detective then says to me, "That's ok, I'm going to go ahead and put the warrant out for your arrest."

At this point, I begin to laugh, and I say to her, "do you have a fax number that I can send you some paperwork?" The detective gives me her fax number and that is when I went to FedEx Kinkos and I faxed her a copy of The Credit Investor Agreement, The Joint Venture Agreement, The Limited Power of Attorney, mail from my credit investors home and a copy of her drivers license and social security card. Needless to say, I never heard anything from that detective again. However, I did find out from a relative of my credit investor that they charged her with filing a false police report.

This is my reason for emphasizing how important contracts and paperwork are when it comes to using a credit investor. And with that being said, I have provided all of the contracts that you will need when dealing with a credit investor.

Contracts And Agreements

The word contract is one of the most powerful words ever created. It comes from the Greek word sustello, which means "to contract" or "to draw together," It can also mean "to shorten" or "to wrap up."

Contracts prevent disputes between all parties involved. At a basic level, contracts are a tool that help businesses, entrepreneurs and people agree more. Since contracts are a collection of terms that parties have reached a consensus on, they are very effective at preventing conflict and contractual disputes in the future. Contracts are so important in business because they provide a clear record of rights, responsibilities, and obligations, thereby ensuring accountability and efficiency in business relationships. They also help maintain compliance. They foster collaboration and communication between two parties. Most of the contracts help generate revenue.

Ultimately the purpose of the contract relates to what it provides, and that is consideration. For contractual purposes, consideration includes the value that has been agreed upon, whether that be an action or item. Property, services, and even protection from harm, are all examples of contractual consideration. Last but not least, the power of a contract is one of the two sides of freedom of contract. On the one hand, freedom of contract is the freedom from restraint, an immunity from legal reprisal for making or receiving promises.

There are four basic elements of a contract. They offer, acceptance, consideration, and intention to create legal relationships.

OFFER: One party makes an offer.

ACCEPTANCE: The other party accepts the offer.

CONSIDERATION: There is an exchange of something of value, such as money, goods, services, or the case of a credit investor, the legal use of their name.

INTENTION: There is a clear intention to create a legally binding agreement.

I have broken down the components and meaning of a contract, so that you will have a clear understanding of the different credit investor documents that I have provided for you in this chapter. Always remember to have multiple copies of any contracts or agreements that you have with any credit investor, and this is especially true for family members. The following pages have every contract and agreement that you will need when dealing with a credit investor.

Letter of Understanding

Date: ________________
ATTN: Prospective Credit Investors

The terms as outlined below shall be defined as a letter of understanding between Credo Company LLC, Inc. and any party interested in serving as an investor for potential/pending real estate acquisitions or refinancing, guaranteeing loans, and backing business ventures with their credit.

Let this serve as a general description of the investor position and transaction terms, specific facts and figures will vary from transaction to transaction and will be agreed upon by all parties as they are presented and secured.

The investor shall present Credo Company LLC, with a mid FICO score of no less than 700 and must apply and meet certain other criteria; specific to obtaining the lender approval based on lender's financing guidelines and criteria. Not every individual with this minimum credit score will qualify, as this may, in some cases, depend on various other factors, including, but not limited to, rent or mortgage history, employment status/history, state of residence, etc.

If approved, investors will not be required to contribute any funds toward the transaction. All closing costs, down payments, appraisals or any other associated fees/cost will be paid by Credo Company, LLC. Its affiliates, clients, and/or from the proceeds of the transaction at closing.

The investor will likely guarantee a company of choice (from Credo Company, LLC). However, if financing is not obtainable in that structure and is required to be held in the name of the Investor, it will be held in the name of the Investor for a period up to 18 months, at which time refinancing or sale of real/personal property shall occur, within a period not to exceed 60 days.

Compensation to the Investor varies from transaction to transaction and will be addressed more specifically as they are presented. Compensation is to be paid at the close of each deal.

______________________________ ____________________

Credo Company, LLC Date

______________________________ ____________________

Prospective Investor Signature Date

BY SIGNING THIS LETTEROF UNDERSTANDING, I ACKNOWLEDGE I HAVE READ AND UNDERSTAND THE GENERAL TERMS AND CONDITIONS OF THIS POSITION AND WISH TO BE CONSIDERED FOR ANY CURRENT AND/OR FUTURE FINANCING ACQUISITIONS FOR WHICH I MAY QUALIFY. I UNDERSTAND THIS WILL INVOLVE OBTAINING A CREDIT REPORT AND MAY REQUIRE PROVIDING FUTHER PERSONAL AND/OR FINANCIAL DOCUMENTATION ON MY BEHALF, OF WHICH I AGREE TO PROVIDE AS REQUESTED.

Joint Venture Agreement

This Agreement made as of the ________ day of ________________, 2025 by and between Credo Company, LLC. C/O Corey P. Smith, (hereinafter referred to as "Credo Company LLC.") and ________________, (hereinafter referred to as "Investor") to form a joint venture.

THAT WHEREAS, Investor, pursuant to the Letter of Understanding dated ________________ has a desire to invest in real estate, guaranteeing loans, business ventures, real property and personal property.

WHEREAS Credo Company LLC is in the business of facilitating investments; and

WHEREAS Investor desires Credo Company LLC to facilitate and administrate investments.

NOW THEREFORE, for and in consideration of the premises and the mutual covenants and conditions hereinafter set forth, the parties hereto agree as follows:

1. General Structure. Investor and Credo Company LL., hereby form a joint venture of which they will purchase the property of ________________ and/or obtain financing for ________________ Credo Company LLC will act as the Contract Administrator for the investment programs entered into by Investor and Credo Company LLC will check the daily operation, subject to terms hereof.
2. Purpose. The purpose of the Venture shall be to invest in ________________
3. Term. This Agreement shall terminate at the consummation of the first and only investment program, however, no later than two (2) years after the date first written above unless otherwise agreed to

by the parties. Notwithstanding any of the above, all monies continuing to accrue from the investment will be distributed to the Venturers according to the following:

(1) First, to pay (or to make provision for the payment of) all creditors of the Venture (including the parties hereto who are the creditors of the Venture) and the expenses of liquidation, in the order of priority provided by law or otherwise, in satisfaction of all debts, liabilities or obligations of the Company due such creditors and such expenses of liquidation;

(2) Second, to the establishment of any reserve which the parties hereto may deem reasonably necessary for any contingent or unforeseen liabilities or obligations of the Venture (such reserve may be paid over by the Parties to an escrow agent acceptable both Parties, to be held for disbursement in payment of any of the aforementioned liabilities and, at the expiration of such period as shall be deemed advisable by the Parties, for distribution of the balance in the manner hereinafter provided in this Paragraph 2); and

(3) Third, after the payment (or the provision for payment) of all debt, liabilities and obligations of the Venture in accordance with clauses (1) and (2) above, to the Parties or their legal representatives in proportion to balances in their respective positive Accounts as adjusted pursuant to Section 5 for all Venture operations up to and including such liquidation no later than the end of the fiscal year in which the Event of Termination occurs or, if later, within 90 days after the date of the liquidation of the Venture.

4. Capital Contributions. (a) The total amount of the capital to be contributed to the Venture shall be given by Credo Company LLC. (b) Investor will provide use of authorized credit to be contributed to the Venture. The investor will not contribute any out-of-pocket funds to the Venture.

5. Net Profits. The Venture's distributable positive net profits will be paid 50% to Investor and 50% to Credo Company LLC. a. The venture shall consist of one (1) eighteen-month (18) month investment program in which Investor shall receive 50% of the profits per investments and Credo Company LLC, shall receive 50% of the profits per investment.
6. Indemnification. Each Venturer (an "Indemnitor') shall indemnify and hold harmless the other Venturer from and against any and all claims, demands, actions and rights of action which shall or may arise by virtue of anything done or permitted to be done by the Indemnitor (directly or through or by agents, employees or other representatives) outside the scope of, or in breach of the terms of, this Agreement. A Venturer who desires to make a claim against an Indemnitor under this Section shall notify the Indemnitor of the claim, demand, action or right of action, which is the basis of such claim, and shall give the Indemnitor a reasonable opportunity to participate in the defense thereof. Failure to give such notice shall not affect the Indemnitor's obligations hereunder, except to the extent of any actual prejudice resulting therefrom.
7. Notices. Except as otherwise specifically provided herein, all notices hereunder shall be in writing and shall be given by registered or certified mail, return receipt requested (prepaid), at the respective addresses set forth below or such other addresses or addresses as may be designated by either party by written notice to the other.

Credo Company LLC ____________________
P.O.Box 11138 ____________________
Memphis, Tennessee 38118 ____________________

8. Entire Agreement. This Agreement supersedes any and all prior negotiations, understandings, and agreements between the parties hereto with respect to the subject matter hereof. Each of the parties acknowledges and agrees that neither party has made any representation or promises in connection with this Agreement, nor the subject matter hereof not contained herein.
9. Modification, Waiver, Illegality. This Agreement may not be canceled, altered, modified, amended or waived, in whole or in part, in any way, except by an instrument in writing signed by all Parties. The waiver by either Party of any breach of this Agreement, in any one or more instances, shall in no way be construed as a waiver of any subsequent breach (whether or not of a similar nature) of this Agreement by the non-breaching Party. If any part of this Agreement shall be held to be void, invalid or unenforceable, it shall not affect the validity of the balance of this Agreement. The Agreement shall be governed by and construed under the laws and judicial decisions of the state of Tennessee.
10. Assignment. Neither Party shall have the right to assign this Agreement or any of its rights hereunder to anyone without the written consent of the non-assigning Party. This Agreement shall inure to the benefit of and be binding upon each of the Parties hereto and their respective successors, assigns, heirs, executors, administrators and legal and personal representatives.
11. Attorney's Fees. In the event of any action, suit or proceeding by either Party against another Party under this Agreement, the prevailing Party shall be entitled to recover reasonable attorney's fees and cost of said action, suit or proceeding.
12. Independent Counsel. The parties hereto understand and agree.

that each has had complete opportunity to have this Agreement reviewed and explained to him/her by independent counsel.

13. Governing Law. The laws of the State of Tennessee shall govern this agreement.

IN WITNESS WHEREOF, the parties hereto have executed this Agreement the day and year first above written.

AGREE AND ACCEPTED:

COREY P. SMITH	MIKE L. MILLER
________________	________________

POWER OF ATTORNEY
(Banking Transactions)

I. Appointment of Attorney-in-Fact

I, [Full Legal Name of Principal], residing at [Address], hereby appoint [Full Legal Name of Agent], residing at [Address], as my true and lawful Attorney-in-Fact.

II. Banking Authority Granted

My Attorney-in-Fact shall have the authority to act for me in all matters relating to my banking and financial affairs, including but not limited to:

- Opening, maintaining, and closing bank accounts in my name;
- Depositing funds into and withdrawing funds from accounts;
- Writing, endorsing, and cashing checks;
- Accessing safe deposit boxes;
- Obtaining bank statements, records, and other financial documents;
- Making electronic transfers, wire transfers, and other transactions;
- Dealing with any bank, credit union, or financial institution on my behalf.

III. Duration

This Power of Attorney shall become effective immediately and remain in effect until revoked in writing by me, or upon my death.

IV. Reliance

All banks and financial institutions may rely upon this Power of Attorney as binding upon me, and they may accept and rely on photocopies or electronic copies of this document.

V. Revocation of Prior Powers

This document revokes any prior Powers of Attorney I have executed for banking purposes.

IN WITNESS WHEREOF, I have executed this Power of Attorney on this ______ day of ______________, 20_____.

____

[Principal's Full Name & Signature]

STATE OF _______________
COUNTY OF _______________

On this ______ day of ______________, 20_____, before me, the undersigned Notary Public, personally appeared [Principal's Name], who proved to me on the basis of satisfactory evidence to be the person whose name is subscribed herein, and acknowledged that they executed the same.

____

Notary Public
My Commission Expires: _______________

POWER OF ATTORNEY

I, [Full Legal Name of Principal], residing at [Address], hereby appoint [Full Legal Name of Agent], residing at [Address], as my true and lawful Attorney-in-Fact.

1. Authority Granted.

My Attorney-in-Fact is authorized to act on my behalf with respect to the purchase, sale, lease, management, and conveyance of real property, including but not limited to:

- Signing purchase agreements, deeds, mortgages, leases, and related instruments;
- Managing closings and escrow accounts;
- Paying necessary fees and taxes;
- Filing and recording documents with appropriate authorities.

2. Property Covered.

This Power of Attorney applies to the following real estate located in [County, State]: [Insert property description or 'any and all real property I may own in the State of X.']

3. Duration.

This Power of Attorney shall become effective immediately and shall remain in effect until revoked in writing or upon my death.

4. Reliance.

All persons dealing with my Attorney-in-Fact may rely on this Power of Attorney as fully binding on me.

In Witness Whereof, I have signed this Power of Attorney on this ______day of ________________, 20______.

____

[Principal's Full Name & Signature]

STATE OF ________________
COUNTY OF ________________

On this ______ day of ________________, 20______, before me, the undersigned Notary Public, personally appeared [Principal's Name], who proved to me on the basis of satisfactory evidence to be the person whose name is subscribed herein, and acknowledged that they executed the same.

____

Notary Public
My Commission Expires: ________________

How To Remove Inquires

This chapter is about removing inquiries, but I want to explain the reason why inquires should be treated as regular accounts, because new technology has enabled banks to get so much information from one simple hard inquiry. You must really do your research to understand what is going on in the world of credit. Let me explain in more detail.

I have heard many people say that credit has changed, or credit repair is dead. That is not true. Think about this, nothing has changed as far as the laws that regulate credit. What I mean by this is derogatory accounts still remain on your credit for seven years, bankruptcy for ten, collection accounts four to six depending on which state that you reside and inquires for two years. You can still file an FTC report or an identity theft report, if you have been the victim of fraud or someone has stolen your identity, and you can still dispute anything that you feel is inaccurate on your credit report and they have thirty days to respond.

What has changed is technology, and because technology has changed it makes it harder for people who were able to use some of the loopholes to repair their credit harder.

The banks have put technology in place such as the (CIP) Customer Identification Program. This is essentially a set of procedures that financial institutions use to verify a customer's identity. They are able to do things like check the security features on a driver's license, such as holograms or watermarks. They can also cross reference customers' information with national databases.

Banks also can use technology such as Plaid. This system utilizes a combination of security measures including strong encryption, multi-factor authentication, and a machine learning model called "Signal" which analyzes users' data to identify suspicious activity and flag potential fraudulent transactions, giving banks the ability to stop ACH transactions and verify bank accounts in real time.

Some of you may be wondering why telephone numbers are so important today, when it comes to being able to get approved or verified by different banking and credit card companies. The banks now use what is called a Voice Response Unit (VRU). This is a computerized phone system that uses recorded messages to interact with callers. This system is also known as Interactive Voice Response (IVR), because it uses AI technology.

This system is closely related to Caller ID Name (CNAM) Lookup, which is technology used to access databases that associate phone numbers with subscriber names, so that banks can verify the phone number is registered to the person applying for credit. My reason for explaining some of the new technology that many of the financial institutions are using now, is because I want you to understand that, if you do not know what is going on within the world of credit or credit repair, YOU CANNOT PLAY THE GAME. Simply put, you got to come with some new tricks.

Many of you do not even understand the history behind why lenders even pull you credit. The "SECRET" behind inquiries lies in their ability to leverage information asymmetry, allowing them to gain valuable insights from experts. This is accomplished by strategically asking targeted questions, often in a two-way conversation where they can benefit from their deep knowledge and perspective, which can be particularly useful in competitive business environments where access to such information might not be readily available to everyone.

But for most people, they think inquiries have little to no influence on their FICO scores. The truth of the matter is sometimes too many inquiries can stop you from being approved for a loan or credit card. When applying for new credit you really do not want more than five total inquiries on your credit report at one time and no more than three in a six-month period.

Banks have even used credit inquiries to discriminate against people based on race, ethnicity, and other factors. This discrimination can lead to lower credit scores, higher foreclosure rates, and limited access to credit. I spoke about this in my book "How to Outsmart The Credit Bureaus."

Some examples of discriminatory credit practices would be Discriminatory data. This is when lenders may use data in scoring systems, such as only counting base salary for some applicants. Credit scoring models are another way for lenders to discriminate against lower income and minority borrowers because information is less accurate in some of these credit scoring models. The one many of you may know about is redlining. Redlining is when lenders have refused or withheld credit to people living in certain areas, often based on race.

The point that I am trying to make is that inquiries do hurt, and you should dispute them in the same manner that you dispute negative accounts. I have provided a way for you to dispute hard inquiries in writing by using the 604 method and by calling the three major credit bureaus and disputing any inquiries that you may have on your credit report. I have also provided letters that you may use to assist you in the disputing process. Following the dispute letters are OPT-OUT Letters to the credit bureaus that will prevent them from sharing your information to third parties or any Affiliate Marketing companies. Just remember that it's very important that you submit these opt-out letters.

Current Date
Your Name
Address
City, State, Zip
Social Security Number
Drivers License Number
Date of Birth

CRA Name
Address
City, State, Zip Code

According to the Fair Credit Reporting Act, Section 609 (a)(1)(A), you are required by Federal law to verify through the physical verification of the original signed consumer contract-any and all accounts you post on a credit report. Otherwise, anyone paying for your reporting services could fax, mail or email in a fraudulent account.

I demand to see Verifiable Proof (an original Consumer Contract with my Signature on it) you have on file for the accounts listed below. Your failure to positively verify these accounts has hurt my ability to obtain credit. Under the FCRA, unverified accounts must be removed and if, you are unable to provide me a copy of verified proof, you must remove the accounts listed below.

Capital One: inquiry date May 14, 2025

I demand the following account(s) be verified or removed immediately.

Name of Account
Date of Inquiry

Provide Physical Verification from Creditor Who Requested Credit

Your Name
Your Address
City, State, Zip

Name of CRA
Address
City, State, Zip Code
Subject: Request To Remove Unauthorized Credit Inquiry
Inquiry Made By:
Inquiry Made On:

To Whom It May Concern,

I am writing to dispute the following information in my file. I recently received a copy of my credit report, and I noticed there is an unauthorized credit inquiry made by the company listed above. To my knowledge, I have not signed any document authorizing the company in question to view my credit report. The listed inquiry was without authorization and for no legitimate business purposes. As such, it is a very serious error in reporting. I never authorized such action, and this constitutes a violation of my rights under the Fair Credit Reporting Act section 604 as well as a violation of my rights to privacy. I am requesting your credit bureau to initiate an investigation and to determine responsible parties in this unauthorized credit inquiry. As part of your investigation, please send the names, business address, and phone numbers of those who made unauthorized credit inquiries so I may contact them directly. In addition, I respectfully request a copy of any document authorizing credit inquiry, and signed on my behalf, so that I may verify its validity.

If you find that I was not the one who authorized this inquiry, I ask that it be removed immediately from my credit file. Please be so kind as to forward me documentation that you have had the unauthorized inquiry removed. If you find that I am in error, then please send me proof of this. Finally, I am requesting an updated copy of my credit report, which should be sent to the address listed above. Your immediate attention to this matter is appreciated.

Sincerely,
Your Name

AFFIDAVIT TO REMOVE FRAUDULENT INQUIRY

Adam Smith
1254 Brookmill Street
Memphis, TN. 38134
Social Security Number:
Date of Birth:

Name of CRA
Address
City, State, Zip Code

Re: Fraudulent Credit Inquiry

To Whom It May Concern:

Recently, I received a copy of my credit report which showed inquiries that I did not authorize. I understand you should not be allowed to put an inquiry on my file unless I have approved it. I have provided you with a police report, and I am currently working with an investigator to stop the use of my name by someone who has stolen my identity. Please have the following inquiries removed from my credit file immediately because I did not authorize them, and they are fraudulent. (List Fraudulent Inquiries)

Macy's 08/21/2025

Also be advised the Fair Credit Reporting Act states that any information that is maintained on an individual's credit report must be accurate. This includes unauthorized inquiries. If your company refuses to investigate and respond to my request within 30 days of the receipt of this certified letter, I am prepared to file a lawsuit in small claims court. Also, be aware that the return receipt/signature of this certified letter is evidence of your receipt of said request.

I have sent this letter because I need your prompt response to this issue, and I need written correspondence as evidence your company is acting upon my request. If you find that I am remised and you do have my authorization to inquire into my credit report, then please send me proof likewise.

____

[signature of affiant]

Adam Smith
1254 Brookmill Street
Memphis, TN. 38134

Subscribed and sworn to before me, this 21st day of September, 2025.

NOTARY SEAL:

____

[signature of Notary]

____

[print name of Notary]

NOTARY PUBLIC
My commission expires:
______________________________, 20______.

Experian Opt-Out Letter

Your Name
Your Address
City, State, ZIP
Date

Experian
Consumer Relations
P.O. Box 4500
Allen, TX 75013

Subject: Opt-Out Request — Affiliate Marketing & Third-Party Sharing

To Whom It May Concern,

I am writing to exercise my rights under the Fair Credit Reporting Act (FCRA), the Gramm–Leach–Bliley Act (GLBA), and any applicable state privacy laws, including the California Consumer Privacy Act (CCPA/CPRA) where relevant.

I formally request that Experian cease sharing my personal information with its affiliates, subsidiaries, or third parties for marketing, promotional, or non-essential purposes. Specifically:

1. I request to opt out of affiliate marketing sharing under the FCRA's affiliate marketing rule.
2. I request to opt out of prescreened credit and insurance offers.
3. If applicable, I invoke my rights under the CCPA/CPRA to opt out of the sale or sharing of my personal information and to limit the use of any sensitive personal information.

Please confirm in writing that my opt-out has been processed and indicate the date it becomes effective.

To verify my identity, I have included:

- Full Name: ____________________
- Date of Birth: ____________________
- Last Four of SSN: ____________________
- Current Address: ____________________
- Previous Address (if within 2 years): ____________________

I appreciate your prompt attention to this matter.

Sincerely,
[Signature]
[Printed Name]

Equifax Opt-Out Letter

Your Name
Your Address
City, State, ZIP
Date

Equifax
Consumer Relations
P.O. Box 740256
Atlanta, GA 30374

Subject: Opt-Out Request — Affiliate Marketing & Third-Party Sharing

To Whom It May Concern,

I am writing to exercise my rights under the Fair Credit Reporting Act (FCRA), the Gramm–Leach–Bliley Act (GLBA), and any applicable state privacy laws, including the California Consumer Privacy Act (CCPA/CPRA) where relevant.

I formally request that Equifax cease sharing my personal information with its affiliates, subsidiaries, or third parties for marketing, promotional, or non-essential purposes. Specifically:

1. I request to opt out of affiliate marketing sharing under the FCRA's affiliate marketing rule.
2. I request to opt out of prescreened credit and insurance offers.
3. If applicable, I invoke my rights under the CCPA/CPRA to opt out of the sale or sharing of my personal information and to limit the use of any sensitive personal information.

Please confirm in writing that my opt-out has been processed and indicate the date it becomes effective.

To verify my identity, I have included:

- Full Name: ______________________________
- Date of Birth: ______________________________
- Last Four of SSN: ______________________________
- Current Address: ______________________________
- Previous Address (if within 2 years): ______________________________

I appreciate your prompt attention to this matter.

Sincerely,
[Signature]
[Printed Name]

TransUnion Opt-Out Letter

Your Name
Your Address
City, State, ZIP
Date

TransUnion
Consumer Relations
P.O. Box 2000
Chester, PA 19016

Subject: Opt-Out Request — Affiliate Marketing & Third-Party Sharing

To Whom It May Concern,

I am writing to exercise my rights under the Fair Credit Reporting Act (FCRA), the Gramm–Leach–Bliley Act (GLBA), and any applicable state privacy laws, including the California Consumer Privacy Act (CCPA/CPRA) where relevant.

I formally request that TransUnion cease sharing my personal information with its affiliates, subsidiaries, or third parties for marketing, promotional, or non-essential purposes. Specifically:

1. I request to opt out of affiliate marketing sharing under the FCRA's affiliate marketing rule.
2. I request to opt out of prescreened credit and insurance offers.
3. If applicable, I invoke my rights under the CCPA/CPRA to opt out of the sale or sharing of my personal information and to limit the use of any sensitive personal information.

Please confirm in writing that my opt-out has been processed and indicate the date it becomes effective.

To verify my identity, I have included:

- Full Name: ________________________________
- Date of Birth: ______________________________
- Last Four of SSN: ___________________________
- Current Address: ____________________________
- Previous Address (if within 2 years): ______________

I appreciate your prompt attention to this matter.

Sincerely,
[Signature]
[Printed Name]

How To Remove Addresses

Many people do not realize the importance of having one address that can be verified. The credit bureaus and banks would like you to believe that addresses are not directly used against you in credit, meaning they do not negatively impact your credit score. They will tell you they are primarily used as identifying information to verify your identity and link you to your credit history. But, not as a factor in determining your credit-worthiness. They may be true, but what you do not know is that a wrong address, a flagged address, or address that is listed in the National Fraud Database fraud can prevent you from getting approved for a loan.

You see the National Fraud Database refers to a centralized system where organizations can share information about suspected fraudulent activity, allowing businesses to check if a potential customer or applicant appears on the database before providing services, essentially verifying their address against a list of known fraudulent locations.

This is why controlling where the mail goes when dealing with a credit investor is very important. And you must also make sure to remove any old addresses, inaccurate addresses, or any addresses that may be in the National Fraud Database.

Whether you are using a physical address or a mailing address, both of them will ultimately get picked up by the three major credit bureaus. These addresses can be reported one of two ways. One way is by a creditor that updates your history monthly or simply by the address that you put on a credit application. Also be mindful that a creditor can also be a collection agency.

Sometime when collection agencies do skip tracing any address that they can find that is associated with you, they will update this information to your credit report even if it is inaccurate. A skip tracers' job is to find someone who does not want to be found. They use whatever is at their disposal, like credit reports, public databases, and paid databases.

If they cannot find you, they will look for family members or friends that you have lived with at some point and time. Keep in mind there are two formats so that collections agencies can update addresses. And they are able to turn off credit bureau reporting using different types of software.

When a creditor or collection agency is uploading an address to the credit bureaus Metro 2 system, they are not allowed to use any punctuation, periods, commas, number signs or any other non-numeric or alphabetic characters. Once again, I want you to really understand the importance of the address on your credit report. Now let's talk about how to remove those addresses that will stop you from being approved.

The first thing that you want to do is change the credit investors address and how you do that is fil out the mail forwarding form from the United States Post Office. Once you fill in that form out, the post office will mail you a form like the one below and you will have to take this form back to any post office once it comes back in the mail. When you go back to the post office, you must take your credit investor, and they must have proper identification. The post office clerk will scan the bar code. This is very important because once this change is made the credit bureaus will automatically add the new address to your credit report. Please examine the change of address form that I have provided.

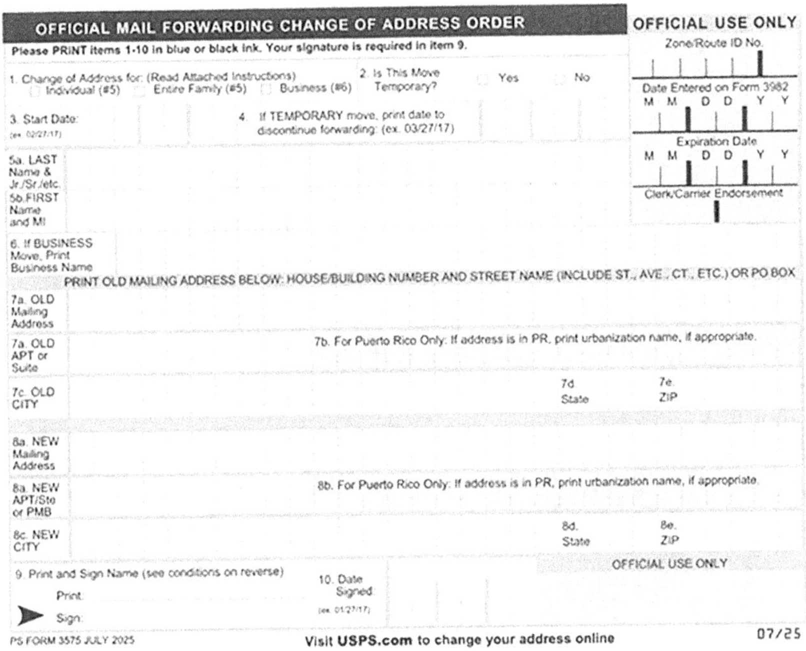

OFFICIAL MAIL FORWARDING CHANGE OF ADDRESS ORDER

Please PRINT items 1-10 in blue or black ink. Your signature is required in item 9.

1. Change of Address for: (Read Attached Instructions) Individual (#5) Entire Family (#5) Business (#6)

2. Is This Move Temporary? Yes No

3. Start Date: (ex. 02/27/17)

4. If TEMPORARY move, print date to discontinue forwarding: (ex. 03/27/17)

5a. LAST Name & Jr./Sr./etc.

5b. FIRST Name and MI

6. If BUSINESS Move, Print Business Name

PRINT OLD MAILING ADDRESS BELOW: HOUSE/BUILDING NUMBER AND STREET NAME (INCLUDE ST., AVE., CT., ETC.) OR PO BOX

7a. OLD Mailing Address

7a. OLD APT or Suite

7b. For Puerto Rico Only: If address is in PR, print urbanization name, if appropriate.

7c. OLD CITY

7d. State

7e. ZIP

8a. NEW Mailing Address

8a. NEW APT/Ste or PMB

8b. For Puerto Rico Only: If address is in PR, print urbanization name, if appropriate.

8c. NEW CITY

8d. State

8e. ZIP

9. Print and Sign Name (see conditions on reverse)

Print:

Sign:

10. Date Signed: (ex. 01/27/17)

OFFICIAL USE ONLY

Zone/Route ID No.

Date Entered on Form 3982 M M D D Y Y

Expiration Date M M D D Y Y

Clerk/Carrier Endorsement

OFFICIAL USE ONLY

PS FORM 3575 JULY 2025

Visit **USPS.com** to change your address online

07/25

The next thing you want to do is get a copy of the credit investors credit report. This can be done either online or by ordering the reports through the mail. After you receive the credit investors reports you want to identify all of the addresses that do not belong on their credit report or any addresses that is connected to a derogatory account.

Once the accounts have been identified, you want to do two things and that is, fill out an FTC fraud affidavit and list the addresses that do not belong on the credit report. I have provided the cover affidavit to attach to the FTC fraud affidavit. Both of these forms must be notarized.

Affidavit For Residential Address

Adam Sand
2343 Danberg Street
Memphis, TN. 32147
Social Security: 423-81-9654
Date of Birth: July 4, 2002

Equifax Information Services
P.O. Box 740256
Atlanta, GA. 30374

To Whom It May Concern:

This letter is to CERTIFY that recently I was reviewing a copy of my Equifax credit report and discovered it contained some errors pertaining to the following "Personal Information." I am requesting that you promptly investigate, update and delete addresses that I never resided and may possibly be listed on my credit report due to fraud. Please see the attached photocopy of my driver's license for your reference. For the record:

1. My name is: Adam Sand, please remove all other name variations IMMEDIATELY. They are not accurate!
2. My current address is: 2343 Danberg Street. Memphis, TN. 32147
3. Please remove all other addresses IMMEDIATELY. I have lived at this address since 04/1994. All other addresses are not accurate.

Please delete these disputed items. Thirty (30) days constitutes a reasonable amount of time for you to complete your investigation. Per the Fair Credit Reporting Act. Please send me notification that these items have been deleted, as well as updated. I hereby acknowledge that the above information is true and correct.

Sincerely,
Adam Sand

____

[Signature of Affiant]
Adam Sand
2343 Danberg Street
Memphis, TN. 32147
Subscribed and sworn to before me, this 8th day of May, 2025.

NOTARY SEAL:

____

[Signature of Notary]

____

[Print Name of Notary]

NOTARY PUBLIC
My commission expires:
______________________________, 20_______

Once you have both of these forms filled out and notarized you must mail them to the addresses below via certified mail ensuring that you know they have been received.

Equifax Information Services
P.O. Box 740256
Atlanta, GA. 30374

Experian
P.O. Box 9701
Allen, TX. 75013

TransUnion
P.O. Box 2000
Chester, PA. 19016

After you know that the dispute affidavits have been received you can then call each credit bureau at the following numbers listed below. The reason why you want to wait until the fraud affidavits have been received is because sometimes the credit bureaus will ask if you have sent in any documentation. All that you have to do is follow the script that I have provided.

All that you have to say is, "I am calling to make sure that the following Fraudulent addresses have been removed from my credit report."

I would also like to add, if you setup online accounts with the three major credit bureaus, sometimes you can automatically dispute addresses that have not been attached to any accounts that are credit or collection accounts.

The Seven Day Credit Sweep Explained

Let me introduce another way that many people are wiping the credit clean, particularly their Transunion credit report. It is known as The Debt Bondage Repair Act (DBRA). The act helps survivors of human trafficking repair their credit by removing negative information from their credit reports. The DBRA is part of the National Defense Authorization Act, which was signed into law by President Joe Biden in December 2021.

Let me explain how survivors use this act to clean their credit.

1.) They must notify the credit reporting agency.
2.) They must provide documentation that verifies that they were a victim of sex trafficking.
3.) They have to submit a request and documentation to the credit reporting agency.

In addition to the information listed above, the victim will have to provide documentation such as proof of identity, such as a driver's license, passport, or birth certificate. They will also need to show proof of their current address, such as a utility bill, bank statement, or insurance statement, and last they will need an Approved Victim Determination Documentation (VDD) from a federal, state, or tribal government entity.

The Consumer Financial Protection Bureau issued a final ruling entitled the prohibition on inclusion of adverse information and consumer reporting in cases of human trafficking. So, the rule prohibits consumer reporting agencies CRA's from reporting adverse credit information resulting from an individuals human trafficking experience. Federal agencies may authorize Non-Governmental Organization (NGO) to provide the documentation that a survivor needs to apply for their adverse information to be blocked.

The program instructions authorized recipients of grants from the office of trafficking and persons to issue trafficking documentation. This ruling was basically designed for victims or survivors of human trafficking, so if your credit was some how impacted as a result of human trafficking, then essentially you can get any of those related items completely removed from your credit report.

The whole purpose of this rule is for individuals who have gone through the experience of human trafficking and have adverse information on their credit reports as a result of being trafficked.

You can also do what is called a self-attestation for human trafficking. This is a document that a person creates to declare themselves a victim of trafficking. It must be signed by a representative from a governmental entity, court, or other authorized organization.

By using the self-attestation technique, a person can still request that information linked to trafficking be blocked from a credit report. Some of the things that need to be included in the statements is the information is true and correct to the best of your knowledge. Also, make sure that you state that you are making the declaration under penalty of perjury. You must include the information that should be blocked, including the source and type of item. Also include dates and account numbers on your document.

One thing that is key when completing this document is that you must have a signature from a representative from a governmental entity, consumer advocacy group, court or authorized NGO. And for those of you who do not know what an NGO is, it is a Non-Governmental Organization (NGO). Examples of NGO's are listed below.

Polaris- An organization that works to create a pathway for survivors.

Lantern Rescue- A non-profit organization that rescues victims of human trafficking and sexual exploitation.

CoMensha- An independent NGO in the Netherlands that works with the police and other agencies to combat human trafficking.

The problem is that many people that are not victims or survivors are using this loophole to get things wiped off their credit report. On the next few pages, I will provide an example of how one individual executed the TransUnion Seven Day Sweep by utilizing the self-attestation process, and by using a Non-Governmental Agency (NGO).

Date: July 29, 2024

SHERMAN OAKS, CA 91423

TRANSUNION, LLC
P.O. BOX 159
WOODLYN, PA 19094

Subject: Self-Attested Request for Blocking of Adverse Information under Regulation V

Dear TRANSUNION, LLC,

I hope this letter finds you well. I am writing to you as a victim of severe trafficking in persons, and I am seeking assistance in compliance with Regulation V, specifically § 1022.142, which addresses the prohibition on including adverse information in consumer reports for individuals like me who have experienced this severe form of trafficking.

SELF ATTESTATION

I, N, attest that I am a victim of severe trafficking in persons, and I have attached the necessary trafficking documentation, as defined under Regulation V § 1022.142(b)(6), to this letter, confirming my status as a trafficking victim.

CRA NOTICE OF LAW

Under Regulation V § 1022.142(c), it is clear that a consumer reporting agency may not furnish a consumer report containing any adverse item of information about a consumer that resulted from a severe form of trafficking in persons if the consumer has provided trafficking documentation to the consumer reporting agency. In light of this regulation, I kindly request that you promptly take action to block the adverse information that is currently included in my consumer report.

ADVERSE ITEMS OF INFORMATION IDENTIFICATION:

Below is a list of the accounts and information that I am requesting to be blocked:

ACCOUNTS:

- **Acct Name: NAVY FCU** - Acct Number: 000143XXXXXXXXXXX
- **Acct Name: BOMBARDIER/CBNA** - Acct Number: 603543XXXXXX
- **Acct Name: ONEMAIN** - Acct Number: 622321XXXXXXXXXX

I attest that the adverse information included in my consumer report is causing me significant distress and further harm. I believe that this blocking request is a crucial step in protecting my rights and privacy as a victim of trafficking.

I understand that Regulation V § 1022.142 requires you to block this information within four business days upon receiving the required trafficking documentation. I kindly request that you adhere to this timeline and provide me with written confirmation once the adverse information has blocked from my consumer report.

Due to significant privacy and data security issues, we request that the Bureau refrains from notifying the mentioned furnishers of the purpose behind the requested blocks. This precaution is necessary to prevent the information from potentially reaching my trafficker and jeopardizing my safety. This request is made in accordance with Regulation V (12 CFR § 1022.82). Your understanding and cooperation in this matter are highly appreciated

Your prompt attention to this matter is greatly appreciated. If you require any additional documentation or information to expedite this process, please do not hesitate to contact me at socialtaxx@gmail.com.

I trust that you will treat this request with the utmost urgency and professionalism, in accordance with the applicable regulations.

Thank you for your cooperation and assistance in this important matter.

Sincerely,

By:______________________________________

All rights reserved UCC 1-308

ENCLOSURES:

- Trafficking Documentation/ Certification
- Driver License
- Copy of SSN
- Utility Bill / Bank Statement

FCRA Section 605C Self-Attestation Form

Human Trafficking Victim Determination Documentation

Survivor's Full Legal Name: ____________________

Social Security Number: ____________________ Date of Birth: ____________________

I attest that I am a victim of trafficking for purposes of Section 605C of the Fair Credit Reporting Act (FCRA).

Under penalty of perjury, I declare (certify, verify or state) that the foregoing is true and correct, to the best of my knowledge.

Survivor's Signature: ____________________ Date: ____________________

To be completed by an individual authorized pursuant to 12 CFR (Code of Federal Regulations) §1022.142(b)(6)(i)(A)(2):

Contact Information for NGO or Anti-Trafficking Task Force:

Organization: ____________________
City: ____________________
County: ____________________
State: ____________________

Representative: ____________________
Position: ____________________
Email: ____________________
Phone: ____________________

I serve with an organization providing services to victims of trafficking, and I attest that the above referenced individual is a victim of trafficking for purposes of Section 605C of the FCRA.

Under penalty of perjury, I declare (certify, verify or state) that the foregoing is true and correct, to the best of my knowledge.

Authorized Personnel Signature: ____________________ Date: ____________________

Page 1 of 1

FCRA Section 605C Self-Attestation Form *Last Revised April 10, 2024*

The Mindset of The Credit Investor

There are many people who do not understand the whole concept of Credit Investor or Credit Partner. Some people have a problem with it because they feel as though you are using the credit investor for personal gain and sometimes the credit investor feels as though you are using them based off of a conversation that they had with someone else.

You must ask the question, who's fault is it when another human being does not know their worth, or they do not understand the power that they have with their name and the advantage they would have in life with the help from outside resources.

And sometimes the thing that stops most individuals is fear, they just do not want to do it, or they want to be told what to do. In my opinion it boils down to the mindset of that person that you are dealing with.

Remember how I discussed the pawn in the game of chess and how it has a short life span. It also told you that the pawn was used to shield more powerful pieces or should I say more powerful people.

There will always be what I call casualty of economic warfare. What do I mean by that you're probably wandering. I mean just as I explained the pawns being used to shield more powerful pieces, therefore sometimes leading to their resource being used by someone else or in the context of the game a much more powerful piece.

You see a "casualty of warfare" refers to any person who is killed, injured, captured, or goes missing during war. It encompasses not just deaths, but also those wounded or taken as prisoners, making "casualty" a broader term.

Now you may be saying to yourself "casualty of war" is a bit extreme while trying to explain credit, but it's not. Most people walk around dead everyday because they refuse to live out their dream, they are captured by their jobs that they hate but cannot quit because their mind is injured with doubt and insecurities about their capabilities. And last, they go missing in war, or should I say life because now there is a much more powerful piece controlling their movements.

Like I said it's a mindset as well. Let me describe the four types of people that exist in this life and the value that they place on themselves. Remember that the value that you place on yourself will ultimately determine your lifestyle and how much money you will earn throughout it.

The lowest level of value is implementation, these are the people who do all the work and make the least amount of money.

The next level of value is management, this simply means that you are managing all the people that are doing the work. So, you are going to make more money than the people that is actually doing all the physical work. These people make anywhere between $50,000 to $200,000.

The next level is communication. Communicators are some of the highest paid people in the world. Communicators transfer information via ideas, words, or spiritual means because it comes from their heart. That is the reason you hear some people say they felt the person who is doing the communication. They make $100,000 to $1,000,000 and they are normally entertainers, actors, singers and even authors.

The highest level of value is imagination. These are people who use their minds to master the people that are using implementation, management, and communication to make money. My point to all of this is, Placing Value on your life means identifying and prioritizing the things that are most important to you, essentially creating a hierarchy of what matters most in your life. At the top of your life should be God, next family, health, integrity and last finance.

You see, truth be told you never want to be a pawn in the game, or believe that your life has no value and most of all you don't ever want to be the credit investor, but you should aim at being one of the most powerful pieces in life and dictate the movement of the credit investor.

www.ingramcontent.com/pod-product-compliance
Lightning Source LLC
LaVergne TN
LVHW050344210926
848481LV00017B/1390